Life-Lifting Devotions for Youth Workers

By Herbert Brokering and Scott C. Noon

Group
Books

Loveland, Colorado

Life-Lifting Devotions for Youth Workers

First Printing

Credits
Edited by Jolene L. Roehlkepartain
Cover designed by Jill Bendykowski
Interior designed by Jill Bendykowski
Cover Illustration by Rand Kruback

Scripture quotations are from the Holy Bible, New International Version. Copyright © 1973, 1978, 1984 International Bible Society. Used by permission of Zondervan Bible Publishers.

Library of Congress Cataloging-in-Publication Data
Brokering, Herbert F.
    Life-lifting devotions for youth workers / by Herbert Brokering and Scott C. Noon
        p.   cm.
    ISBN 0-931529-79-4
    1. Church work with teenagers—Prayer-books and devotions-English. I. Noon, Scott C., 1960-   . II. Title.
BV4596.Y68B76   1990
242'.692—dc20   90-36514
                                                              CIP
Printed in the United States of America

From Herbert:

To my family
who incarnates the gifts
of the spirit.

From Scott:

To the person who has taught me
most about "devotion"—
my wife, Becky.

Contents

Introduction 6

Youth Ministry With a Reason...8
The Miracle of Growth 10
Breaking Bad News to Parents 12
Success Struggles 14
Working Together as a Team 16
Transitions 18
Living the Compassionate Life 20
Those Hardest to Love 22
A Web of Support 24
Your Youth Ministry Budget..26
Dreams and Visions..28
Assessing People's Needs...30
Growing Older...32
Setting Goals 34
Thanksliving..36
Boosting Your Self-Confidence 38
Graduation Goodbyes 40
Flops and Failures...42
A Well-Rounded Youth Ministry.......................................44
From Junior to Senior High..46
A Welcome Place 48
Recreation and Re-Creation...50
When You Love Too Much 52

Different Gifts, Different Vocations................54

Short on Time 56

Beyond Crayons................58

Bored With Youth Group 60

Recognizing Volunteers 62

Stretching Your Limits................64

The Perfect Youth Minister................66

Your Sexuality 68

Taking Time for Kids................70

Finding Family Time................72

Frustrations and Broken Dreams 74

Giving Away Your Ministry 76

Reaching Unchurched Kids................78

Are You Listening? 80

The Healing of Forgiveness 82

Your Cup Runneth Out................84

Your Teenage Years................86

Keeping Confidences................88

Team Ministry................90

Mission Statements................92

Living a Life of Shoulds................94

The Kid Who Hates You 96

Ministering to Parents................98

Dealing With Differences 100

Positive Discipline................102

Top Priority 104

Your Christian Lifestyle................106

Introduction

It's not easy working with teenagers. Whether you're a full-time youth minister or a volunteer, you feel the pressures of balancing budgets, meeting needs, developing creative programs and juggling a hectic schedule.

At times you may become exhausted and spiritually dried up. *Life-Lifting Devotions for Youth Workers* refreshes your soul and renews your energy for ministry. You'll find 50 interactive devotions that specifically address your personal and professional concerns.

Herbert Brokering, poet and author of more than 30 books, crafted the beginning thought and ending prayer for each devotion. Scott C. Noon, a full-time minister to youth and their families, wrote the "Read," "Think" and "Do" sections. Together their talents have made this book rich with reflection, insight and practicality.

Each devotion includes five parts:

● **Reflect**—A parable, poem or thought that guides you to look at life from a new, fresh perspective.

● **Read**—Key scripture verses and additional readings to help you discover how God's Word relates to your ministry.

● **Think**—Thought-provoking questions to help you think of the devotional topic in a new way.

● **Do**—Ideas for putting your new insights into action in your personal life and ministry.

● **Pray**—Conversations with the Creator that encourage you to deepen your personal prayer life.

Side by side with your appointment book, *Life-Lifting Devotions for Youth Workers* will encourage and build you and your youth ministry.

So when you're feeling the pressure, take time for some personal devotions. And you'll begin to see the pressures you face in your ministry in new, refreshing ways.

———————

God, there is pressure.
It can crush down, it can unfold a seed.
God, there is pressure.
It can make me faint, it can give me energy.
God, there is pressure.
It can wear me down, it can pull me up.
God, there is pressure.
It can slam a door, it can fly a kite.
God, there is pressure.
It can swear, it can sing.
God, there is pressure.
It can feed a headache, it can smell a rose.
Amen.

Youth Ministry With a Reason

They drew the picture of a call.

Some drew a voice.

Some drew a bugle.

Some drew a bell.

Some drew a shepherd.

Read

"Then I heard the voice of the Lord saying, 'Whom shall I send? And who will go for us?' And I said, 'Here am I. Send me!' " (Isaiah 6:8).

Also read: Exodus 3:1-14; 1 Samuel 3:1-10; and Isaiah 6:1-8.

Think

● How has God sent you into youth ministry? Do you see your youth ministry as a calling? What doubts do you face about whether you've been "called"? How do you constructively address those doubts?

● Why do people enter youth ministry? Is there a single motivation? How does God use and shape our ill motivations? our good motivations?

Do

● Start a journal about your "call." Write how God led you to youth ministry.

● Talk to three people you're close to in your church. Ask them to honestly evaluate your ministry and your effectiveness as a youth minister.

Pray

Lord, ask me.
Get me used to questions.
Raise my curiosity.
Help me peek.
Give me a glimpse.
Get me into the interrogative mood.
Put me to a test.
Let me qualify.
Give me a choice.
Make me choose.
Lord, ask me. Amen.

The Miracle of Growth

There was a town
where the people lost their strength.
The young dozed by noon,
and workers nodded on their way to the fields.
The yawning began it all.
Yawning was like a disease,
and it spread through all the people.
A visitor came to waken them all.
Seed would surely waken them all.
Every day where they went
there was seed.
Sometimes it was food.
Sometimes it wrestled with the sun or thistles.
Sometimes it took deep root.
Always it was at work.
The seed never yawned,
and it was filled with great strength.
The sower stayed until all signs of yawning left,
and the town grew well and wide awake.

Read

"Still other seed fell on good soil. It came up, grew and produced a crop, multiplying thirty, sixty, or even a hundred times" (Mark 4:8).

Also read: Proverbs 27:23-27 and Mark 4:1-20.

Think

● As you consider the parable of the sower, do you find the most seeds of faith in good soil, rocky soil, thorny ground or along the path?

● How does a youth worker play the role of farmer in preparing the soil to receive the seed and grow?

● What's your role as a youth worker in helping people who are caught on the path? on rocks? in the weeds?

Do

● Go into a garden and snatch a cup of dirt. Plant some seeds in the soil and watch them grow over the next few weeks. Observe the growth and draw conclusions about personal spiritual growth.

● Think of four young people; one being trampled on the path, one caught in the weeds of the world, one languishing from a lack of love, and one growing in good soil. Be a bit of sun and nourishment to them by sending them each a note of encouragement.

Pray

Lord,
if there is such determination
hid in a seed,
then
no wind will blow me away
before I take root. Amen.

Breaking Bad News to Parents

Once there was very bad news
that had to be told,
and there was no getting around it.
The one who would tell it
knew there were steps
to heal those who would hear the news.
After steps of denial,
anger
and grieving,
there would come acceptance.
It is so in all the world.
Good Friday finds Easter
on the third day.

Read

"Instead, speaking the truth in love, we will in all things grow up into him who is the Head, that is, Christ" (Ephesians 4:15).

Also read: Genesis 19:1-26 and Ephesians 4:11-15.

Think

● How do you speak the truth in love to parents? What does it mean to be open and truthful with parents?

● When parents ask about their teenager's participation and behavior, how honest are you? When parents don't ask, do you ever tell them what their teenager is like? Why or why not?

● When an accident happens, how do you break the bad news to parents? How can you make these situations easier?

Do

● Phone four parents. Ask them for feedback on how you've communicated tough issues and emergencies. Ask how you could improve.

● Make a checklist of what you'd say to parents in an emergency. Do you have necessary medical information for each teenager? If not, get it. Do you know first aid? If not, take a first-aid course in your community.

Pray

Lord, when I'm breaking bad news
*   prepare me to join a broken family.*
Lord, when I'm breaking bad news
*   make me quiet.*
Lord, when I'm breaking bad news
*   promise me the power to recover.*
Lord, when I'm breaking bad news
*   open my lips and heart together.*
Lord, when I'm breaking bad news
*   heal me through a new relationship. Amen.*

Success Struggles

There once was a man of success,
you could tell by his manner of dress,
with a towel in his hand
and a crown as headband
there was no one he tried to impress.

His mind was never on greed,
he accepted as scepter, a reed.
In the man's greatest hour
seven words were his power,
connecting his thought, word and deed.

Read

"O Lord, let your ear be attentive to the prayer of this your servant and to the prayer of your servants who delight in revering your name. Give your servant success today by granting him favor in the presence of this man" (Nehemiah 1:11).

Also read: 1 Samuel 18:14-15 and Psalm 118:24-29.

Think

● Who gives and determines our success? How is the Holy Spirit responsible for what you accomplish?

● How do you define success in youth ministry? How is faithfulness to your call determined with regard to success?

Do

● Draw a coat of arms for a successful youth worker. Make a shield and divide it into six parts. On the left half of the shield, include words or symbols for the following three areas: qualities that make a youth worker successful to parents; qualities that make a youth worker appealing to teenagers and qualities that identify a successful youth worker among fellow professionals. On the right half of the shield, use symbols or words to show the results of these qualities.

● Reread the poem on page 14. What does it say to you about youth ministry and success? What attitude should you have toward success?

Pray

O God, you lead us.
You call us.
You draw us up.
You create a right spirit within us.
When we are driven, it is another spirit.
When we are drawn, it is your Holy Spirit. Amen.

Working Together as a Team

Once a people wished to work together
in a way to conserve their energy.
They voted to watch each other each week
and write whatever they did well.
Each Monday they shared their lists,
which were always true.
From the long lists of items
they chose those they would do together.
There was little duplication of work
and a great saving of energy.
Everything on the list counted,
and often very tiny items
proved most productive.

Read

"From him the whole body, joined and held together by every supporting ligament, grows and builds itself up in love, as each part does its work" (Ephesians 4:16).

Also read: 1 Kings 19:19-21 and Luke 22:24-34.

Think

● How does the biblical image of the body influence your thinking about teamwork? How does the body, both physically and as the church, work together toward a goal?

● Why did the disciples need to work together as a team? How did teamwork enable their ministry? How did fighting disable their ministry? How do you and your volunteers work together as a team?

Do

● With your volunteers, build a human machine involving as many people as possible. Only allow two hands and three feet to touch the ground. Otherwise everyone must be off the ground. Work together!

● Fold a paper airplane with only one hand. How does the cooperation of your two hands serve as an example of teamwork?

Pray

God, when we test each other,
*   show us the value of one another.*
When we test each other,
*   show us where we are strong.*
When we test each other,
*   show us a greater potential.*
When we test each other,
*   show us how we are united.*
God, when we test each other,
*   show us your strength. Amen.*

Transitions

Once there was a girl who knew many secrets.
She developed a system by which
she disguised everything she did well.
No one could copy or even know
exactly what she had discovered.
She produced many systems
for much information,
and many hired her.
Everything she did was done
so no one else could ever do it again
or take it from her.
So disguised was what she did
that many wondered and marveled.
She never collaborated,
and no one created anything with her.
When she moved,
people had no way of contacting her
for she left no address.
Since then, people have forgotten her name.

Read

"As he was praying, the appearance of his face changed, and his clothes became as bright as a flash of lightning" (Luke 9:29).

Also read: Matthew 3:17—4:11 and Mark 1:11-14.

Think

● As Jesus changed physically in the Transfiguration, how was he undergoing transition? How different was Jesus' ministry before and after the Transfiguration?

● What transitions are you facing in your life right now? How is your ministry changing? Who has helped you survive those changes?

Do

● Make a file called "Affirmations." In it, keep all the notes from parents, pastors, kids and others who've expressed appreciation to you. Keep the file handy for those difficult transition times.

● Prepare a file that contains the many details of your ministry. Include event evaluations, volunteers' names and telephone numbers, places with church charge accounts, van and bus rental companies and area recreation centers. Then if you're ill, on vacation or if you leave your ministry, your replacement will have the information.

Pray

God, when I move on,
    will I have left a legacy?
When I move on,
    will I have blessed the person who follows?
When I move on,
    will I have my eyes on you?
When I move on,
    will I move on?
God, when I move on,
    will I say thanks? Amen.

Living the Compassionate Life

What do I ask the poor
so I can learn from them about Jesus?

What do I ask the prisoners
so I may learn from them about Jesus?

What do I ask my enemies
so I will learn from them about Jesus?

What do I ask
to learn about Jesus?

Read

"This is what the Lord Almighty says: 'Administer true justice; show mercy and compassion to one another. Do not oppress the widow or the fatherless, the alien or the poor. In your hearts do not think evil of each other' " (Zechariah 7:9-10).

Also read: Matthew 5:1-12 and 19:16-26.

Think

● How does God command you to practice compassion in your ministry? Which teenagers need your compassion the most?

● How do you become a good role model for compassion? How do you teach teenagers to become more compassionate?

Do

● Research ways you and your young people can serve others in your community. Serve in one of these ministries this week.

● Challenge yourself to a simpler lifestyle. This week have one or more meatless meals. Fast for a meal or two. Prepare a bag lunch rather than going out to lunch. Use the money or time you save to help those in need.

Pray

Lord, I lost my crucifix;
*   can I find it in a hunger line?*
Lord, I lost my silver-plated cross;
*   can I find it in a prison?*
Lord, I lost my painting of Gethsemane;
*   can I find it in a rehab center?*
Lord, I lost your face;
*   can I find it in a stranger? Amen.*

Those Hardest to Love

A woman who grew African violets
went door to door
giving each family a plant slip
to root and keep alive.
People held their breath for weeks
as the slips rooted and grew.
The woman then called the people together
to understand what they had done.
They saw a great difference in their spirit
and felt their patience had increased.
All knew the delicate nature and beauty
of the African violet.
The woman was thankful for this experiment
for the child in need of great love and patience
lived in her house
with all the violets.

Read

"Love is patient, love is kind" (1 Corinthians 13:4a).
Also read: Romans 7:14-25 and 1 John 4:7-10.

Think

● When you get frustrated and angry, how do you regain your patience? How does a loving attitude help you with kids who are hard to love?

● How can you love a hardened teenager into a new style of relating?

Do

● Think of kids in your youth group who challenge you—the loudmouth, the one who talks back, the apathetic teenager. This week, spend time with one of them, call two of them and jot a note to the rest saying, "I was thinking about you today."

● Write a skit about a troubled teenager who finds hope in an adult who won't give up on him or her.

Pray

Lord, my patience seems to be so weak,
and love is running low.
My voice has lost its laughing sound,
and joy has lost its glow.

If you can turn the summer heat
into a winter snow,
then you can warm my heart some more,
and give it back its glow.

If patience is a gift you give
and that is all I need,
then keep my eye upon the sun,
the rain, the earth, the seed. Amen.

A Web of Support

Once upon a time
when things fell apart for people,
they watched the spider make the web.
A world unfolded
and from within the spider
came what was needed to make a webbed universe.
It glistened in the sun,
and what was once only space
became a city of many streets and alleys.
The dining room of the spider
was in the center of this great metropolitan network.
Those staring for a long while
learned that within the spider
was the knowledge to create a world
of tiny threads.
So the people began to see lines between places
that were no longer empty spaces,
and their network became great.
And in the middle of it all,
they ate together.

Read

"Make every effort to keep the unity of the Spirit through the bond of peace" (Ephesians 4:3).
Also read: 1 Corinthians 12:1-31 and 3 John 1:5-8.

Think

● How do you keep the unity of the spirit through the bond of peace? How is networking with other churches an expression of unity in Christ?

● Is your ministry well connected with other youth ministries? How would activities with other churches help or hinder your own ministry? How would contact with other youth workers help or hinder your own ministry?

Do

● In the yellow pages, find other churches in your area. Contact them and arrange to meet at least a couple of youth ministers from these churches. When you meet, discuss the joys and challenges of youth work and swap activity ideas.

● Draw your web of support. Start with a small circle in the center for yourself. With additional lines and circles, attach other networks you're a part of, such as volunteer organizations and social groups. Then list the resources each group possesses that could help your ministry.

Pray

O God of desert sand and lily pond,
of deepest thought and stars beyond,
keep us connected in our space
as we and others interface.

O God of all we say and see,
help us know what we can be;
in all the things we will embrace
keep us connected to your grace. Amen.

Your Youth Ministry Budget

They couldn't afford what they needed
so they looked at the world in another way.
They marked places with the sign of the cross,
and said the places were theirs to borrow.
They needed space
so they found it in each other's homes.
They needed new stories
so they visited the aging.
They needed a playground
so they walked to a park.
They needed a project
so they rescued a pond.
They needed a place to dance
so they met on the street.
They needed a banquet
so they each brought a casserole and a candle.
There was no budget for them at this time.
So they found these and many gifts
for which there was no charge.

Read

"Of what use is money in the hand of a fool, since he has no desire to get wisdom?" (Proverbs 17:16).

Also read: 2 Chronicles 31:2-21 and 1 Peter 5:1-4.

Think

● Why is it important to be wise about money? What does the presence or absence of money teach us about ministry?

● What's the relationship between bigger budgets and better ministry? What factors contribute to a good relationship between bigger budgets and better ministry? What factors make the relationship insignificant?

Do

● Prepare a dream budget for next year. Between the lines of the budget, describe the ministries the money would enable. Include goals in these descriptions as well.

● Show your budget to a few church board members. Use their reactions to alter your "dream" before submitting the real request.

Pray

Lord, for every gift and prize,
large and small and middle-size,
gifts that make us kind and wise,
we give you thanks; we give you thanks.

Lord, for every gift we need,
wind and sun and sea and seed,
gifts of thought and word and deed,
we give you thanks; we give you thanks. Amen

Dreams and Visions

What they liked most of all
were homemade biscuits,
topped with a little honey.
What they liked even more
were sentences from scripture,
scrolled and baked inside each biscuit.
They called it vision bread.
Since they'd agreed to all the sacred words
that would go into the biscuits each month,
they were never disappointed.
Each scroll gave them a vision,
and they saw God's Word in a new way.
Through the years they ate many biscuits,
and saw many dreams.
They grew,
and their vision increased.

Read

"One night the Lord spoke to Paul in a vision: 'Do not be afraid; keep on speaking; do not be silent. For I am with you, and no one is going to attack and harm you, because I have many people in this city'" (Acts 18:9-10).
Also read: Joel 2:28-32 and Acts 16:9-15.

Think

● How do you notice God's presence with you? Does it enable you to move onward, or does it make you more aware of the realities you face?

● What are the limits of your youth ministry vision? Money? Time? Volunteers? Other commitments? How can you overcome these limits?

Do

● Play soft music and sit in a comfortable chair. Take an imaginary journey with Christ as he leads you through an unknown valley to a high cliff. As you look into the valley below, you see a lot of teenagers. Some are dying—by self-starvation, chemical dependency or self-hatred. Others are waist-deep in mud, symbolizing the conflict in their lives.

As you look off the other side of the cliff into an adjacent valley you see a much smaller group of young people who know their lives have purpose. Your meditation concludes when Jesus asks, "How will we get the young people out of the first valley, over this mountaintop and into the second valley?"

● List everything you'd do if you had ample money, time and volunteers. Work on the most unrealistic option.

Pray

Lord of promise, Lord of hope,
dreams and visions, jumping rope,
hook my mind and inner eye
on a word you magnify. Amen.

Assessing People's Needs

Once a shepherd carried both rod and staff.
The rod was for pressing sheep to the ground,
to examine them for wounds
as they entered the sheepfold.
The shepherd held them tight,
poured oil where wounds were open.
And as the sheep scampered into the fold,
the shepherd called the sheep by name.
Every sheep was examined with care
and there were none that could not be wounded
and made well.

Read

"And my God will meet all your needs according to his glorious riches in Christ Jesus" (Philippians 4:19).

Also read: Mark 14:32-42 and Luke 9:12-17.

Think

● How does God meet all your needs? In your ministry, are your needs more, less or as important as your kids' needs?

● What needs do your young people have? Which ones do they realize? Which needs are harder to get teenagers to examine?

● What special needs do teenagers in your community have? How can your church reach out to those young people?

Do

● Contact three youth-serving agencies in your area. Find out how your church can help young people in a new and creative way.

● Tour your community with a camera. Photograph people who depict various needs in the community. Then choose one photograph each day, and pray for guidance in meeting the needs of people in that photograph.

Pray

God, help us where we hurt.
Hear us when we holler.
Save us when we sink.
Lift us when we fall.
Feed us when we hunger.
Hold us when we cry.
God, help us when we hurt. Amen.

Growing Older

She was young;

the young identified with her.

She was in a university;

the young visited her at homecoming.

She went to work;

the young asked her for a tour through the company.

She was married;

the young talked to her about love.

She bore a child;

the young discussed childbirth.

She became famous;

the young bought her book.

She was sick;

the young caroled in the hospital.

She retired;

the young invited her to a banquet.

She was old;

the young asked her to tell old stories.

She became senile;

the young hugged her.

She was buried;

the young sang about eternal life.

At every age, she was active with the young.

Read

"They will still bear fruit in old age, they will stay fresh and green" (Psalm 92:14).

Also read: Isaiah 46:4 and Lamentations 3:4.

Think

● How can fruit be borne in old age? Is the same true of youth workers? Can youth workers be fruitful when they're 40? 50? 60? 70? 80?

● When was the last time you came home sore from a youth activity? Is youth ministry only for young people?

● How can being young enhance your ministry? detract from it? What if you're old?

Do

● On separate index cards, write one quality of an effective youth minister. Then in the top right-hand corner of each card, mark an "X" for qualities that improve with age and an "O" for qualities that decline with age. Now answer the question: Do youth ministers become more or less effective with age?

● Make a life-line. On a sheet of paper, draw a horizontal line representing your life. Designate various ages along the line. What gifts have you experienced at various ages in your life? What gifts do you anticipate? How might these gifts be used in youth ministry?

Pray

God, I am always a person. Amen.

Setting Goals

Once when people wanted to be new

and in tune with their souls,

they agreed to a way of rebirth.

At an agreed time,

they laid down and became quiet,

curled up as when they were very tiny.

Under some soft light they laid most still.

They pictured themselves in rebirth

traveling into all—and through all—into God.

They were in the center of all that is God's.

They do it at least once each year.

Read

"I press on toward the goal to win the prize for which God has called me heavenward in Christ Jesus" (Philippians 3:14).

Also read: Nehemiah 2:17-18 and Acts 2:16-21.

Think

● What goal has God set before you toward which you "press on"? How is this goal a part of your youth ministry?

● As you dream about the year ahead, how do you envision your ministry? How will you be faithful to your call from Christ over the next few years?

● What about your family? What personal family goals would you like to establish? How can you balance your family time and your ministry?

Do

● Walk through your church with your eyes blind-folded. As you go on your tour, realize how much you depend on vision. After your "travels," write a vision for your ministry and yourself for the coming year. Post your vision near your desk as a guideline for your work and your programming.

● Read a good book about personal development. Use its ideas to improve your ministry.

Pray

God, you hold the pieces together.
What scatters returns in another harvest.
The tides come back to the center.
Homing birds don't lose their way.
Our soul knows a way.
There is a pathway.
There are your signs.
God, we are guided. Amen.

Thanksliving

Once
a prince took off his royal robes
to become a beggar.
His hair grew, as did his nails.
He bent mightily as he leaned to look
where he walked,
and the sack on his back was often heavy
at the end of the long day.
He bowed when he begged and when he received.
At dusk and dark each day, it was clear to him,
all he had was what he had received.
And so through the years
what he had never said as a prince,
he learned to say as a beggar:
Thanks.
Thanks.
His body was badly bent,
and his spirit grew upright.

Read

"I thank my God every time I remember you. In all my prayers for all of you, I always pray with joy because of your partnership in the gospel from the first day until now" (Philippians 1:3-5).

Also read: Luke 17:11-19 and 1 Thessalonians 5:12-23.

Think

● How do you express your thanks to and for your partners in youth ministry? How do you remain thankful as you serve Christ?

● What people in your past have encouraged and supported you in your ministry? Do they know how they nurtured you?

Do

● Write teenagers and volunteers each a short, personal note saying what you appreciate about them and why.

● Throw a thanksgiving feast for your teenagers and tell them how much you appreciate knowing them.

Pray

God, if thanksgiving and feelings of grace
fill my body and my space,
just how does it show
so that others will know? Amen.

Boosting Your Self-Confidence

*Once there was a child who listened to others
who told her she was dumb, stupid, ugly, mean.
She heard it so often through the years
she believed it.
Whenever she went to church
she listened to the sermon
and sang the hymns,
but she could never understand them
because they didn't say these words about her.
She couldn't read the Bible
for she couldn't believe the words of God.
Instead she believed the words of the people
who said she was dumb, stupid, ugly, mean.
Someday she'll understand the Bible,
and she won't believe the words of those
who say she is mean, ugly, stupid and dumb.
Perhaps someday she'll help them feel
beautiful, smart and good.*

Read

"Even though I walk through the valley of the shadow of death, I will fear no evil, for you are with me" (Psalm 23:4a).

Also read: Psalm 27; Jeremiah 1:4-10; and Luke 18:9-14.

Think

● What is your confidence like when you walk through the valley of the shadow of death? How does knowing that God is always with you give you confidence?

● When is your confidence the best? the worst? Is your self-esteem usually based on others' feelings? your own feelings? God's?

Do

● Write a "self-confidence creed." Include all the positive things you believe about yourself. List your best qualities, strengths and special abilities. Read it to yourself each day this week.

● Get out newsprint and markers. Draw a full-length picture of yourself. In the picture, symbolize the many gifts you possess. Draw them in appropriate places on the picture. For example, draw a telephone by your ear for your ability to listen.

Pray

Lord, when I'm afraid,
   touch me.
When I'm silent,
   be an ear.
When I sink,
   be a rock.
When I cry out,
   be an altar.
Lord, when I need to hear the truth,
   be the amen. Amen.

Graduation Goodbyes

When a child was very young,

his father went into the big doorway of the airplane.

The child pressed his face

against the smoky window of the airport,

and cried "Daddy! Daddy! Daddy!"

It was the child's first powerful goodbye.

The mother stood behind and watched the pain and fear.

As the child grew older,

he recalled the fierce and powerful words

"Daddy! Daddy! Daddy!"

And as the child went and came,

the mother stood with the father,

saying those old words: "Goodbye. Goodbye. Goodbye.

Hello. Hello. Hello."

These are the words buried deep in every child.

These are the words by which we learn

the wonder of waiting.

These are the words by which the church was born:

The one you see leaving will come again.

Read

"If one of you says to him, 'Go, I wish you well; keep warm and well fed,' but does nothing about his physical needs, what good is it?" (James 2:16).

Also read: Luke 15:11-32 and James 4:9.

Think

● Does James 2:16 suggest that when you say good-bye to a graduating group member, your responsibilities to that person end? If not, what responsibilities continue?

● What's your ministry role to graduating students? to their parents? How do you enable them to be connected to the church after they move on?

Do

● Recognize graduating seniors' school accomplishments and youth group contributions. Have a banquet and give gifts of appreciation.

● Encourage graduating seniors who'll remain in town to get involved in other ministries of the church. Encourage them to volunteer in the nursery or join the young-adult group.

Pray

O Christ, give us a sense of great presence
with those who leave us
and a closeness that transcends
living in the same room. Amen.

Flops and Failures

Once upon a time

there were young men filled with a hope

that was hidden deep within them.

Most of them were known

as people who failed,

and much was said against them.

Then a stranger came to their town,

and chose them from all the others.

By their wounds, it was evident who they were

and in them there was a great hope

that most did not see.

Each day the young men met

to find the wounds and scars deep inside themselves.

For some it was hard

to talk about their other side.

They could not easily find

the words and pictures to get

to the other side of their wounds.

So they practiced climbing through barrels,

wading through deep water,

rummaging through old attics,

and sky diving through the air.

They practiced going through what they could.

And they found ways to get to the other side.

Read

"For all have sinned and fall short of the glory of God" (Romans 3:23).

Also read: Proverbs 15:22 and Romans 3:21—4:8.

Think

● According to scripture, who can expect to flop? How can God work with and through our flops?

● Is there a pattern to your flops? For example, does a lack of sleep make you flop-prone? Or do you fly off the handle when volunteers don't keep their commitments?

Do

● Draw two vertical lines on a sheet of paper to divide it into three sections. In the first column, list your greatest flops. In the second column, list the damage that resulted from each mistake. In the third column, write what you learned from each mistake. How damaging to your ministry were these mistakes? How was the learning worthwhile?

● Find a bandage. On it, write a scripture verse that encourages you when you fail. Hang the bandage on your bulletin board.

Pray

Upon the hill, the awesome tree
we find the cross of Calvary
and then your silent victory
O God of scars and mars. Amen.

A Well-Rounded Youth Ministry

Once a family grew up on a farm
in the middle of a field.
The house had windows on every side,
and the children knew the weather patterns
that came from every direction.
Now they are ministers.
They know all seasons of the year by heart.
When they think of Easter,
they remember Good Friday.
When they think of sounds,
they think of all the senses.
When they think of heaven,
they think of Earth and all the seas.
When they think of Christ,
they think of all the saints and of the universe.
Anything reminds them of everything.

Read

"Hear my prayer, O Lord, listen to my cry for help; be not deaf to my weeping. For I dwell with you as an alien, a stranger, as all my fathers were" (Psalm 39:12).

Also read: Mark 6:31-32 and John 6:5-13.

Think

● What needs are being met in these scriptures? Does the Bible address only spiritual needs? How important is it to meet emotional, intellectual, physical, social and spiritual needs?

● How important is a balanced youth ministry? What happens when ministries focus on just one or two needs?

Do

● Dig up a list of activities your youth ministry has offered during the past year. Divide your events into the following five growth categories: emotional, intellectual, physical, social and spiritual. How balanced was your ministry? What changes will you make?

● Survey your young people. Determine what needs your teenagers have in each of the five areas. For example, you may find that some teenagers could benefit from an aerobics class. List potential programs in each of the five areas.

Pray

Lord of sights and touch and sound,
skies and seas and wind and ground,
help me look at every space,
in your wondrous living place.
Lord of mercy all around;
make me holy in the round. Amen.

From Junior to Senior High

In the day of Jesus

the distance between classes was known.

The rich kept their distance.

The Pharisees kept their distance.

The poor had their distance.

The lepers knew their distance.

It was a law that they stay apart,

one arm's length from the others.

Jesus broke that law

and touched them all.

Read

"Therefore let us leave the elementary teachings about Christ and go on to maturity" (Hebrews 6:1a).

Also read: 1 Samuel 3:1-10 and Luke 2:43-52.

Think

● How does your youth ministry help young people "go on to maturity"? How do you offer more responsibilities as teenagers grow older?

● How does your program cater to senior highers' needs? How do you address their concerns such as jobs and extracurricular activities?

Do

● Interview three junior highers and three senior highers. Have them describe the various challenges in their lives. Ask them what they want from the church. Note the differences between what the senior highers and junior highers say, and implement them into your ministry.

● Visit a junior high school and a senior high school. (Check visiting policies first.) Watch the differences in teaching methods and teenagers.

Pray

God, everything is on the move.
Winter goes into the summer.
Babies become toddlers.
Cement turns into runways.
An introduction turns into a relationship.
Summer warms the winter energy.
The young reshape inheritance.
Adolescents sort through emotions.
God, everything is on the move. Amen.

A Welcome Place

The children walked with the minister through the church.

They stood in every room,

touched the cross, the altar,

every chair and every sign on the wall.

Each time they touched something,

and liked it very much,

the minister said, "It belongs to you."

The children now own stained-glass windows

too large for their homes,

and organ pipes they cannot count.

They believe the minister who said, "It belongs to you."

The children are teaching this to the older people.

All who join this church inherit a great wealth.

Read

"And as she stood behind him at his feet weeping, she began to wet his feet with her tears. Then she wiped them with her hair, kissed them and poured perfume on them" (Luke 7:38).

Also read: Genesis 18:2-8 and Matthew 9:9-12.

Think

● Why was washing people's feet an important symbol of welcome in biblical times? What comfort and relief came from foot-washing? How does your church offer the same sense of welcome and comfort?

● Why is it important for youth groups to invite and welcome people? What makes your youth ministry attractive to guests?

Do

● Analyze your youth group meeting room. Does it feel like the teenagers' room or just another church room? How can you make it a welcome place for kids?

● Meet with your teenage leaders and ask if they believe the youth ministry is *their* youth ministry. What changes can you make so it belongs to them?

Pray

O God, show us the signs of welcome in our worship.
Help us stand together, turn toward each other,
　　sing in harmony,
eat the same bread, kneel side by side,
　　wave, meet another's eyes,
recognize a voice, say a name by heart,
　　speak in unison,
intercede for each other, give thanks,
　　hear the same readings,
　　hug, and join in a three-fold amen.
O God, show us signs of how we welcome one another.
Amen.

Recreation and Re-Creation

Once those feeling weak gathered
to look at their bodies as energy.
They saw energy in cell chemistry, muscles,
DNA patterns, nerve synapses, electrical impulses,
brain waves, heart rhythms.
They saw in themselves a great moving force,
a power, a dynamo.
And so they came on the great notion
of energy conserved, stored, transformed,
released, converted.
Now they meet more and more often
to be transformed, restored, released.
Some call these meetings Dynamite.
Some call them Force.
Some call them Spirit.

Read

Praise the Lord "who satisfies your desires with good things so that your youth is renewed like the eagle's" (Psalm 103:5).

Also read: John 2:1-10.

Think

● How does God satisfy your desires and renew you? How do you get away from the busyness long enough for renewal?

● What is the role of recreation in re-creation? How is play an important part of youth ministry?

Do

● Review your schedule for the past six months. How much time did you devote to personal recreation? Make a commitment to meet your needs for exercise and physical renewal.

● Create a recreation directory for your area. Include area activity centers, parks, baseball diamonds, swimming pools and game areas. Plan ways to include recreation in your ministry.

Pray

O God, your earth wants to heal,
  and make life new.
Ponds want to heal
  and become our drink.
Trees want to heal
  and bear us fruit.
Minds want to heal
  and make us glad.
Souls want to heal
  and convert.
O God, you are the healer. Amen.

When You Love Too Much

Sometimes we lock ourselves in.

Sometimes we lock ourselves out.

A circle can be too tight.

A circle can be too large.

We live between a center and circumference.

The one in us is the one around us.

We lean in; we lean out.

Read

"We love because he first loved us" (1 John 4:19).
Also read: Luke 9:24 and 1 John 4:7-21.

Think

● How do you define God's love, love for yourself and love for others? How do you balance loving yourself, loving God and loving others?

● When have you loved someone so much that the relationship became unhealthy? Is it healthy when young people rely totally on you? How can you shift your relationships so kids become more self-reliant?

Do

● Go to the library and learn about co-dependence. Find out how it affects families, particularly those facing alcoholism or other addictions. How can you help families in these situations?

● On paper, draw a large circle. On the inside, write what you believe is a reasonable, basic job description for yourself, both at work and at home. Outside the circle, describe things that go beyond what's healthy for you or your ministry. Include maximum work hours, minimum time for peers and social contacts, minimum time for yourself and minimum time for family. Use the drawing to set personal guidelines.

Pray

God, there's a prison full of kind people.
  They are heroic, special, sacrificial, doing good.
  They are admired, thanked, applauded,
and yet they feel they are in prison.
  They don't yet see the prison bars.
  They don't know they hold the key.
God, the lock is on the inside. Amen.

Different Gifts, Different Vocations

There is a professor

who sees all of life as a fraction.

He can see

the numerator and the common denominator at once.

Each year he chooses a new numerator;

they are his gifts.

The common denominator is the same

through all the years.

The common denominator is Christ.

The professor divides Christ into each gift;

Christ fractures the gift

to break it into tiny pieces

and there's even more.

As the talent is divided by Christ,

the professor multiplies.

Read

"Are all apostles? Are all prophets? Are all teachers? Do all work miracles? Do all have gifts of healing? Do all speak in tongues? Do all interpret? But eagerly desire the greater gifts" (1 Corinthians 12:29-31).

Also read: 1 Corinthians 12 and 14.

Think

● Why does God give people different gifts? What gifts has God given you? How do you seek God's will in your ministry?

● What do you teach young people about different vocations? about choosing a college? How can you help teenagers find God's will?

Do

● Reread 1 Corinthians 12:4-11. Circle the gifts in the passage you believe God has given you. Write names of others in your church who have other gifts mentioned. Think of ways you can better use your gifts in ministry while also encouraging others to use their gifts.

● Create a college and career center in your church. Ask a volunteer to keep the center up to date with college catalogues, career information, handbooks from technical or trade schools, armed services pamphlets and mission opportunities.

Pray

God, you have one voice
and many tones.
You have one voice
and many languages.
You have one voice
and many words.
God, make clear your voice. Amen.

Short on Time

Once there were those
who ran out of time.
They went looking for more.
In the Bible, they found much time.
On every page they read time words— "suddenly,"
"after he had left," "early in the morning,"
"then," "while they were waiting."
They looked at trees and gardens,
and all that grew was old or new
or blooming or bearing fruit or dormant.
In everything that grew, they found time.
They looked at seasons and found different speeds of time.
Sometimes time was sudden.
Sometimes time crept in and was too slow to notice.
For everything was time, and of time,
and they were always in the middle of all kinds of time.
All they could do was enjoy time more fully
and be in awe at the wonder of time.

Read

"There is a time for everything, and a season for every activity under heaven" (Ecclesiastes 3:1).

Also read: Ecclesiastes 3:1-11 and Isaiah 40:12.

Think

● How can there be a time for everything when it seems there's never enough time? Does time shape your ministry, or does ministry shape your time?

● What time crunches do you feel? Does your ministry need more of your time? Does your family? Do individual teenagers? What percentage of your work hours should be allotted for each?

Do

● Set an alarm clock to ring 30 minutes from now. When it rings, evaluate your own working style. Do you tend to let interruptions throw you off track? Do you skip from project to project? Do you group similar projects together? Determine and eliminate time-wasters.

● Spend a day off without a watch, clock or schedule—without worrying about what time it is. How does it feel not to watch the time? How does that change your concentration? your heartbeat? What do you learn about yourself and your schedule from this activity?

Pray

O God, how did you ever think of creating time? Amen.

Beyond Crayons

Once an old man
saw a great new coloring book.
So big was this book with large pictures of Jesus
that he bought huge crayons
with which to color the pages.
He'd been a farmer for 40 years
and knew the colors in the nativity.
With his large crayons,
which he grasped with his calloused grip,
he colored the straw purple
for it was a royal bed.
He colored the donkey black with gold trim
for it was a royal rider.
He colored the swaddling clothes
the seven colors of the rainbow
for they made a most royal robe.
He did not color the nativity for how it looked,
but he colored it for what the nativity is.
He went beyond the crayons,
and he didn't stay inside the lines.
When people saw what he had done
they came from afar
for he was awesome.

Read

"In the beginning was the Word, and the Word was with God, and the Word was God. Through Him all things were made" (John 1:1, 3a).

Also read: Genesis 1:1—2:9 and Matthew 25:14-29.

Think

● How does God continue to create in the world? Where does the inspiration for creativity come from?

● How can you challenge and nurture your own creativity? How can you encourage creativity in your teenagers and volunteers? What aspects of your youth ministry could be enhanced with more creativity?

Do

● Challenge your creativity. Plan a far-out issue of your youth newsletter. Write a skit for your youth group. Rewrite words to a hymn.

● Blow up some balloons. On each one, write something you've created. Celebrate your creations by batting the balloons around your office.

Pray

O God, your spirit orders chaos.
Shake us up,
*   and put us together.*
Turn us around,
*   and point the new way.*
Send us your muses,
*   and give us brand new laughter.*
When we stop,
*   give us your word.*
When our line is too hard,
*   bend it. Amen.*

Bored With Youth Group

It's the same thing over and over.

Same old place.

Let's change the place.

Same old time.

Let's change the time.

Same old way of seeing things.

Let's change that. With a candle.

Let's put a candle outside—in a garden,

on the steps, in an alley, under a tree, in a parking lot.

And celebrate those places,

and see what's going on.

What if a wind blows out the flame?

We'll put it in a pumpkin.

What if it's winter?

We'll carry it.

Just light the candle.

And look around. Listen around. Feel around.

Imagine around. Wish around.

Something happens when a candle is lit.

The candle shows that something is already happening.

And we can see it.

You can never run out of places to set candles.

Never.

There are plenty of places.

Just get enough candles.

Read

"Do you not know? Have you not heard? The Lord is the everlasting God, the Creator of the ends of the earth. He will not grow tired or weary, and his understanding no one can fathom" (Isaiah 40:28).

Also read: Exodus 32; Isaiah 40:28-31; and Hebrews 12:3.

Think

● Scripture suggests that God never gets bored. How do you tap into this source of renewal? How can God help you when you're bored?

● What do you need to keep your creative juices flowing? Continuing education? reading? a regular day off? Add some of these activities into your schedule.

Do

● Stand in front of a mirror. Make faces that show boredom. What do you see? How do these faces make you feel? Now make faces that show you're interested in something. What's different?

● Save one afternoon for apathy-busting. Dive into creative resources. Brainstorm with friends. Take a candle to a place you've never gone before and think of how you could have a youth group meeting there.

Pray

O God, help us see a lot in a little.
Through a word, show us a conversation.
Through a song, show us a festival.
Through a thought, show us a friend.
Through a problem, show us a possibility.
Through a seed, show us a blossom.
Through a desert, show us a water hole.
Through darkness, show us a candle. Amen.

Recognizing Volunteers

There once was an altar of stone;
a person did kneel there alone.
In a night of ill-will,
rang the words, "Yes, I will!"
The altar is now a high throne.

Read

"My heart is with Israel's princes, with the willing volunteers among the people. Praise the Lord!" (Judges 5:9).

Also read: 2 Corinthians 6:1-10 and Hebrews 2:17—3:4.

Think

● Why would Deborah and Barak refer to willing volunteers as the princes of Israel? How do they resemble leaders of God's chosen people?

● How has volunteering in your youth program enhanced the spiritual journey of your volunteers? What opportunities do you provide for them to grow in their ministry skills and their faith?

Do

● From memory, list all your volunteers. Then check your list against an actual volunteer listing. Who did you miss? If you remembered them all, which two did you think of last? Call each "forgotten" volunteer, and take him or her to lunch. If you have fewer than four volunteers, take them all to lunch.

● Plan a dinner to recognize your volunteers for their hard work. Involve kids by having them prepare speeches, write letters, send invitations and serve the meal.

Pray

O God, you gave us your name: "I Am."
In your name
    give us the power to say "I will."
In your name
    give us the desire to say "I am able."
O God, you are our namesake. Amen.

Stretching Your Limits

Everything can be seen mathematically.

We learned it when little.

When we played we divided and subtracted.

We added and multiplied

with sand and toys and crackers.

Show and tell was only the beginning.

There is so much to see, feel, smell, taste.

There is so much to walk on, swim in, climb, eat.

There is so much to read, write, hear, sing.

There is so much out there.

There is so much inside.

Every time we add a piece of information,

everything in us changes.

And there is no end to the change.

And no beginning.

God said "Let there be!"

And there is.

There sure is.

Read

"Forgetting what is behind and straining toward what is ahead, I press on toward the goal to win the prize for which God has called me heavenward in Christ Jesus" (Philippians 3:13b-14).

Also read: 1 Corinthians 9:24-27 and Philippians 3:12-16.

Think

● Why does the scripture say to forget what is behind and strain toward what is ahead? What makes you press forward?

● What quality would you like to develop in yourself? What goals do you need to set to achieve growth in this area?

Do

● Stretch a rubber band. What happens? When you're stretched, how do you feel? How can you deal with the joy and pain when you're being stretched?

● Pick your favorite hymn. Add a new verse by using the theme "going that extra mile for God."

Pray

Lord, there's always more.
We burn a forest, and the green returns.
We give up, and someone else begins.
We forget what we wanted to say,
and a new thought comes to mind.
Everything can heal.
Everything can transform.
Everything can be renewed.
Life can rise again.
Lord, there's always more.
Show us how much there is. Amen.

The Perfect Youth Minister

They had two ways of looking.

One looked as she went along the way.

She tried to do everything

and to do it perfectly.

The other looked only to the end of the road.

He always tried to get there

and to do it perfectly.

Whether they went slow or fast,

they tried for perfection.

So there were these two:

One saw what was growing along the path.

The other saw where the path led.

Then the two became friends.

They are learning from each other,

to walk together.

They are seeing more and more along the way.

There is so much to do.

They are learning the length of the road.

There is so much ahead.

Now there is no time for either to be perfect.

Their lives are full

of what is going on

and what is ahead.

Read

"Do not conform any longer to the pattern of this world, but be transformed by the renewing of your mind. Then you will be able to test and approve what God's will is—his good, pleasing and perfect will" (Romans 12:2).

Also read: Matthew 5:48 and Philippians 2:5-11.

Think

● How does God describe "perfection"? How does the world? How are the two different? What's the difference between being perfect at what you do and being faithful?

● How does perfectionism push you to burn out or work all the time?

Do

● Draw a characterization of the perfect youth worker. Is the description attainable? How perfect is your drawing?

● The next time a volunteer or teenager puts together a less-than-perfect program, monitor how you react. Do you try to save the program? Allow it to have rough edges?

Pray

O God, take us to the garden
  where we can kneel
  and say "Your will be done."
Take us to the garden
  where we can kneel
  and hear "He goes ahead of you."
O God, take us to the garden
  where we can kneel
  so we can stand on our own. Amen.

Your Sexuality

Once a child noticed, without knowing how,
that everything had a playmate.
The sun had a shadow.
The wind had a silent calm.
The seed tried to snuggle itself into earth.
The moon had a dark side.
Laughter followed crying.
Bumble bees liked nectar and pollen.
People held hands.
And opposites hurried off to be married.
It seemed very good and simple,
until the child grew
and discovered that holding hands is a choice.
Opposites choose each other.
The sun is too strong for some plants.
And there's a time and season for everything.
The child learned quickly
that everything is chosen to fit the other
so it won't be crushed or hurt
but to live together for a very long time.

Read

"Create in me a pure heart, O God, and renew a steadfast spirit within me" (Psalm 51:10).

Also read: Psalm 51:10-17 and John 8:3-11.

Think

● In what ways do you need God's help to create a clean heart in you?

● How does your sexuality impact your ministry? How do married and single youth ministers approach youth ministry differently?

● How do you handle your own personal attractions? How do you handle kids who are attracted to you?

Do

● List times you've either felt attracted to a teenager or a teenager had a crush on you. Create a checklist for handling these attractions when similar situations arise.

● Consult a counselor or social worker about transference. Find out what he or she does when confronted with his or her own affections or other people's.

Pray

God, in me is a person who can grow
    through this day and year
    into eternal life.
As I have chosen against all odds
    to be,
so help me choose against all odds
    to be a person. Amen.

Taking Time for Kids

Once a land ran out of paper.
There could be no more printed agendas
or note pads to jot on what to do.
So the land watched the children.
They always knew what to do next
just by being where they were.
If they were in water,
the water seemed to say what to do.
So it was with the sand,
a tree or a steep hill.
By watching the children,
the land learned to do what there is to do.
And when there is paper again,
the land will still watch the children.
The land watching children
will know what to do.

Read

"But Jesus called the children to him and said, 'Let the little children come to me, and do not hinder them, for the kingdom of God belongs to such as these'" (Luke 18:16).

Also read: Matthew 9:9-12 and Romans 12:16.

Think

● Why was Jesus so open to young people? Why would God turn over the kingdom to kids? What about them makes them special in God's eyes?

● Is it difficult to tear yourself away from planning and paperwork to spend time with teenagers? Why take time to be with kids?

Do

● Spend time with three different kids this week. Meet them after school or over the weekend for at least an hour. Eat ice cream. Check out the mall. Swim at the pool. Do whatever you like.

● Devise a weekly visitation list that helps you connect with your kids more often.

Pray

God, you never go away.
You stay, for there is enough here.
You stay, for you see all the connections.
You stay, for you see more and more.
You stay, for you watch the children.
You stay, for you know how it began.
You stay, for you recognize the value.
God, you stay and never leave. Amen.

Finding Family Time

God is sometimes mother,
uncle, grandma, brother.
God is sometimes sister,
shepherd, queen or mister.
God is close relation
inside all creation.

Read

"If anyone does not know how to manage his own family, how can he take care of God's church?" (1 Timothy 3:5).

Also read: Galatians 6:10 and Ephesians 5:31—6:4.

Think

● What's the relationship between the call to your church and the call to your family? How do these two callings intersect?

● How do you model healthy family life?

● What priority did Jesus place on his family? What priority do you place on your family?

Do

● Spend three hours at one time with your family at least three days this week. Have a special time with each member of your family.

● Think of a person who has no family. Do something to brighten that person's day. For example, invite him or her over for dinner or go shopping together.

Pray

O God, bless our floor plan
Make our living room
    your nave.
Make our kitchen
    your sacristy.
Make our porch
    your narthex.
Make our table
    your altar.
Make our door
    your aisle.
Make our conversation
    your lectern.
Make us your chancel. Amen.

Frustrations and Broken Dreams

Once he used paste and glue.

Now he welded as a hobby.

They brought metal to the room,

and with each piece they told a story of woe.

There were parts of bicycles and autos.

They brought bent screwdrivers and twisted wire.

In the room was far more metal than they expected,

and the stories ran long.

Fenders and bumpers were too large

to fit a final sculpture,

and he cut these with electric cutting rods

into many shapes and pieces.

From this heap of metal scraps,

he welded flowers with iron petals and sharp leaves,

and left them covered with a white cloth.

In the morning when he had gone

those who gathered saw their souvenirs of woe

standing in the sun

as an iron bouquet.

They called it "Iron Easter."

Read

"All his days he eats in darkness, with great frustration, affliction and anger" (Ecclesiastes 5:17).

Also read: Job 6:11—7:3 and Romans 8:20-28.

Think

● Why does someone who's frustrated eat in darkness? How are darkness and frustration alike?

● How prone are you to frustration? What are your prime sources of frustration? How can you address them?

Do

● Grab a piece of cold charcoal from a grill. Rub it in your hands as you think about your frustrations. Think about the mess you make while you stew over your frustrations. Then, as you wash your hands, think of ways you can get rid of frustrations before they make a mess, such as taking a walk or talking with someone about them.

● Write your frustrations on slips of paper. Then put all those frustrations in a gallon-size reclosable bag. Seal the bag, but leave room to insert a straw. Blow air into the bag. Then slip out the straw, seal the bag and use it to punch away your frustrations!

Pray

O God, give us a party.
Make it out of leftovers.
You be the host.
Let us fly our frustrations
on a long string in your spirit wind.
O God, be the life of our party. Amen.

Giving Away Your Ministry

A little can be a lot more
if the little is divided by four
so think of the root
you'll find in the fruit
if you open the fruit to the core.

There's a power when people divide
to break open the things that they hide
when they learn how to give
there's far more they'll live
as the pieces of parts coincide.

Read

"So if you consider me a partner, welcome him as you would welcome me" (Philemon 1:17).

Also read: John 20:19-23 and Acts 2:1-21.

Think

● How are your volunteers partners in your ministry? How do you give away aspects of your ministry?

● What are your "delegating tendencies"? Do you delegate whole projects or simple tasks? Do you give responsibility and authority with each task? Is it easy for you to delegate? Why or why not?

Do

● Look at your list of "things to do." What everyday tasks could you delegate to a teenager or volunteer?

● List everything you've delegated in the past few weeks. Add up the total hours it took everyone to do all the tasks. Think of the total hours as the amount your ministry has multiplied through delegation. Celebrate by treating yourself to a favorite dessert or a relaxing time listening to your favorite music album.

Pray

O God, of the sea and the earth,
show me how subdividing increases my worth. Amen.

Reaching Unchurched Kids

Once in a land of lakes and desert sand

people skipped pebbles on the water.

Each stone cut into the water

and touched off a circle

of tiny waves and ripples.

One of the young filled with understanding

who watched them throw pebbles,

said it was a picture of the church.

A science teacher standing there

summed it all in the following way:

The work of the church is a centrifugal force,

sending out circles from the center.

When the farthest wave has touched a distant shore,

the energy returns,

and the waves move back to the point of contact.

The work of the church is centripetal.

Christ is the rock.

Some say the church reaches out, and then reaches in.

Some call it mission.

Some call it outreach.

Some call it breathing.

Some call it evangelism.

Some call it living.

Some call it skipping pebbles.

Read

"Therefore go and make disciples of all nations, baptizing them in the name of the Father and of the Son and of the Holy Spirit, and teaching them to obey everything I have commanded you. And surely, I am with you always, to the very end of the age" (Matthew 28:19-20).

Also read: Colossians 4:2-6 and 1 Timothy 3:1-9.

Think

● How does Christ's command to share the good news prompt you to invite newcomers? How well has your church followed this command?

● Examine your attitude toward newcomers. With limited hours, a tight budget and a busy schedule, is outreach a priority for you? How can you create a more positive approach to outreach?

Do

● Develop a "bring a friend" program. Focus on celebrating friendship. Choose a location that's non-threatening to newcomers, such as a community center, YMCA or school facility.

● Imagine you're an unchurched kid who knows nothing about your youth ministry. Is the youth newsletter written in "insider" language? Is the youth room easy to find? Can you meet people at meetings? Will someone contact you after the meeting? If so, who?

Pray

O God, you know the story;
you know each line;
the story is theirs
and isn't just mine.
O God, you know the story
of sand on the shore,
and when we stop walking,
there's still a lot more. Amen.

Are You Listening?

They lived together.
He was blind from an accident.
She didn't hear well.
While she spoke, his eyes would open.
He listened as though to see.

She learned to talk as though he saw,
and it helped her hearing.
She learned to speak to his inner eyes.
With her words, she shaped trees, colored sights,
painted smiles and traced tears.
She spoke with all her senses,
and he saw deeply and far.

When he listened to her, he saw.
So through the years, he taught her to see,
and she taught him to listen.
In their weaknesses lay their strength.
They healed each other.

Read

"He who answers before listening—that is his folly and his shame" (Proverbs 18:13).

Also read: 1 Samuel 3:1-10 and Luke 10:38-42.

Think

● Why does the Bible advise people to listen before talking? Why is this still good advice?

● Does your prayer life include listening? Why or why not? How could you learn to listen better?

Do

● Listen to music with headphones. Now try to do your work, including telephone calls, without taking off the headphones. How important is it to listen clearly and fully? How can distractions ruin communication?

● This week notice how much time you spend listening and talking. See if you can identify any patterns. Then spend 20 minutes listening to the sounds around you.

Pray

O God, show me the smells of the seasons.
Show me the emotions of the children.
Show me the needs of a friend.
Show me the riches of the poor.
Show me the sights inside silence.
Show me how to see when you speak.
Show me, O God, show me. Amen.

The Healing of Forgiveness

Forgive.

Let's find it in Webster's.

It comes just after the word forge.

Just after forget-me-not.

Webster's. Forge: a furnace or hearth

where metals are heated.

Forge: a workshop

where pig iron is transformed into wrought iron.

Forge: to form by heating and hammering into shape.

Forge.

It's a good word in Webster's, just before the word

forgive.

Forgive: to excuse for a fault or offense; to pardon.

Forgive: to renounce anger or resentment against.

Forgive: to absolve payment of.

Forgive: to free the offender from the consequences.

Forgive: to pass over a mistake or fault

without demanding a punishment.

Read

"This is my blood of the covenant, which is poured out for many for the forgiveness of sins" (Matthew 26:28).
Also read: Psalm 130 and Matthew 26:26-30.

Think

● Why did Jesus give his blood to forgive us? What does that say about forgiveness?

● How do you model forgiveness and reconciliation in your ministry? If forgiveness is so healing, why is it so difficult to do?

Do

● Ask someone to lock you in a closet for a short while. Experience the separation from others, the stopped communication. How is being released healing? renewing? How is it like forgiveness?

● Use a concordance to do a word study of forgiveness in the Bible. Think of specific ways you can implement in your ministry the forgiveness you read about in each passage.

Pray

Lord, look the other way.
Waive.
Release.
Nullify.
Delete.
Let me off the hook, Lord.
Clear the books, Lord.
Harbor no grudge, Lord.
Let bygones be bygones. Amen.

Your Cup Runneth Out

Some touched the hem of Jesus' garment,
and power left him.
Jesus lifted up his face,
and the power was replenished.

Read

"But Jesus often withdrew to lonely places and prayed" (Luke 5:16).

Also read: Luke 6:12-19.

Think

● Why did Jesus withdraw to lonely places to pray? What does it say about how he handled stress? What role does prayer play in avoiding burnout?

● What steps do you take to balance people time with program time? alone time with people time? work time with family time? vacation time with work time?

Do

● Light a match. As it burns, notice its properties. See how dry and lifeless it becomes. Notice how the high heat burns away some of the original material. How does this illustrate the times when you're burned out?

● Go through your calendar and mark days off in advance for family time and alone time. When people ask for appointments, just say "I already have a commitment."

Pray

O Lord,
why did you go off alone?
How did you get through the crowd?
Where did you go to kneel?
What did you leave unsaid?
How much did you leave undone?
O Lord,
why did you go off alone? Amen.

Your Teenage Years

Once a woman began to write
when she was very little.
She saved her first words and pictures
and new diaries that followed.
She saved her term papers and her letters.
They're all in a box called, "Teens."
She is still a writer,
and in that box lie the characters
for her many novels,
and for the stories she tells at family reunions.
Some of the people who scared her most
when she was little
are now favorite characters in her children's stories.
She has learned to face all her old enemies.
And she has remembered her friends.

Read

"Remember not the sins of my youth and my rebellious ways; according to your love remember me, for you are good, O Lord" (Psalm 25:7).

Also read: Genesis 3:1-14 and Luke 2:41-50.

Think

● Why does the psalmist ask God to forget the sins from the past? What were the sins of your teenage years? How was God's forgiveness part of your healing that helped you become who you are today?

● When you were a teenager, what gave you the greatest joy? the greatest pain? What frustrations did you have? What successes did you achieve? What feelings did you have toward school? church? your family?

Do

● Review photo albums from your teenage years. Identify how God worked in your life. Make a photo collage and keep it as a reminder of some of the same feelings your young people may be going through.

● Borrow a teenager's yearbook. Lay it next to your yearbook. How was your life like that teenager's life? How was it different? What challenges are the same? How can you minister to teenagers today?

Pray

God, I am full of wonder.
I am full of maps where I have been.
I am full of emotions that mingle.
I am full of faces that fly like balloons.
I am full of rhythms that march like parades.
I am full of sights that can flood galleries.
I am full of joy that makes me speechless.
God, I am full of wonder. Amen.

Keeping Confidences

People once began to notice

that nothing was startling anyone.

There was a shortage of secrets

and nothing of great importance was being said

that needed confidence.

Everything was in the open.

No one whispered,

and no one confessed behind closed doors.

It was a disease.

The only cure was for people

to close doors, tell true stories,

look quietly at one another,

and promise forgiveness.

As people began to say, "I'm sorry,"

and startle one another in secret,

the disease was cured.

Curiosity and wonder returned.

Read

"Now it is required that those who have been given a trust must prove faithful" (1 Corinthians 4:2).

Also read: Micah 7:5 and 1 Corinthians 4:1-5.

Think

● Why does God say those who've been given trust must prove faithful? Why is confidentiality such an important trust?

● Do your young people trust you? Why or why not? How do you show you can be trusted with confidences?

● How do you avoid breaking confidences? When should confidences be broken? When does confidentiality involve more than keeping secrets?

Do

● Consult a lawyer or your local Child Protection Services to find out what issues you must report. For example, every state requires that all child abuse cases be reported, even by clergy.

● Discuss your church's expectations regarding confidentiality with your senior pastor or church board. Then write a policy statement about confidentiality. Ask your church board to adopt it, then publish it so everyone clearly understands it.

Pray

O God, how far does truth go?
When is it time for someone else to know?
How much should someone tell me?
What am I willing to hear?
O God, what do I do with the truth? Amen.

Team Ministry

A tree can only live

in an environment.

A word can only live

in a context.

A baby will only live

in an embrace.

A thought will only live

if received.

A human can only live

in a family.

A noun can only live

with a predicate.

I can only live

in community.

Read

"From him the whole body, joined and held together by every supporting ligament, grows and builds itself up in love, as each part does its work" (Ephesians 4:16).

Also read: Exodus 4:10-16 and Acts 13:42-50.

Think

● How does your team ministry hold together? work together?

● What can Moses and Aaron teach us about team ministry? Paul and Barnabas? How does a team balance strengths and weaknesses? What strengths will your associates need to balance your weaknesses? What gifts will you contribute to enable their work?

Do

● Invite your youth ministry team members and their spouses or guests to a party or dinner. Build fellowship with creative team-building games.

● During a meeting with your volunteers, have the group form a close circle. Have people each turn to face the back of the person next to them. Then have them do a "lap-sit" where people each put their hands on the shoulders of the person in front of them and slowly sit down together. Then discuss how a team must work together.

Pray

God, sometimes put me in the middle
to surround me.
Sometimes put me under
to overwhelm me.
Sometimes put me alongside
to strengthen me.
Sometimes put me behind
to lead me.
Sometimes put me out
to draw me in. Amen.

Mission Statements

*Once a congregation of many groups
made a deck of many cards.
On each card was the name of one group.
Each week the people met to deal the deck,
and for seven days each dealt deeply
in some unforgettable way
with the group on the card drawn.
Each week they returned the card
to draw another.
The cards became the mission.
And the people became a body
of all the parts of the church.*

Read

"For a long time now—to this very day—you have not deserted your brothers but have carried out the mission the Lord your God gave you" (Joshua 22:3).

Also read: Luke 10:1-12.

Think

● What mission has God given you? How do you allow God to shape the direction in which your personal mission will go? How do you take responsibility for shaping the mission of your youth ministry?

● What objectives does your ministry try to accomplish? What is the goal of your work with young people?

Do

● Write a mission statement for your overall youth ministry. Include your target audience and the purpose of your ministry. Then write a mission statement for each of your smaller ministries. For example, write separate statements for your junior high youth group, your senior high group and the youth choir. Carefully define the mission of each group.

● Listen to the theme song from the television series *Mission: Impossible.* How does the driving beat make you think your youth ministry mission *is* possible?

Pray

O God you call me, and I am sent.
You lead me, and I am compelled.
You convince me, and I am committed.
You hold me to it, and I am freed.
You ask me, and I know what to say.
O God, you have a way of keeping all things going.
Amen.

Living a Life of Shoulds

Should is the past tense of shall.

Should obligates us.

Shall indicates the future

and declares us able.

Read

"In the same way, the Spirit helps us in our weakness. We do not know what we ought to pray for, but the Spirit himself intercedes for us with groans that words cannot express" (Romans 8:26).

Also read: Exodus 20:1-17 and 1 Corinthians 13:9-13.

Think

● How does the Spirit intercede for you? Why is the Spirit so important?

● Why is it tempting to impose a lot of shoulds to improve ourselves?

● What are all the shoulds you impose on yourself? How does this pressure influence your life of faith?

Do

● Write each of your "shoulds" on separate index cards. Keep one or two that you want to act on. Burn the rest.

● Buy a helium balloon. Use it as a symbol of one of the "shoulds" you want to give to God. Then go outside and release it into the air.

Pray

God, you made me your own,
I shall not want.
You say I am able,
I shall not put myself down.
You call me your own,
I shall not see myself as unworthy.
You make all things new,
I shall count on it.
God, you are my savior.
I shall not want. Amen.

The Kid Who Hates You

Once there was a way of looking
that never took offense.
Those who learned about this way
found it in someone who'd been tormented,
jeered, spit upon, whipped and left hanging
on a tree in a hot afternoon.
The anger of enemies was reflected
'til they saw their own hate mirrored
in the one on the tree.
Whatever they did couldn't change the person's love.
They were surprised by prayers of forgiveness.
They'd wanted to be liked,
and while screaming and hostile
they found they were loved.
They learned from the one who saw them
from the top of a green tree.
It was a way of looking.

Read

"If anyone says, 'I love God,' yet hates his brother, he is a liar. For anyone who does not love his brother, whom he has seen, cannot love God, whom he has not seen" (1 John 4:20).

Also read: Proverbs 15:1; 21:14; and 1 John 2:8-12.

Think

● What teenagers have you had a hard time liking? How does God want us to handle personality conflicts?

● How do you handle a teenager who hates you and leaves the church? How do you handle a young person who seems out to get you?

Do

● Spend time this week with that teenager who hates you. Talk about your differences. Get to know each other a little better. Write the teenager's name on a card and keep it in your pocket. Pray for him or her each day.

● Make an appointment with a school teacher to discuss handling personality conflicts. Does the teacher confront conflicts openly or ignore them? What are the results? What can you learn from his or her approach?

Pray

God, I need a crucifix.
When I'm turned away, I see you there.
When I feel hostile, I see you there.
When I'm rejected, I see you there.
When I'm not heard, I see you there.
God, I need the crucifix,
*   so I can yell and stay loved.*
God, I need the crucifix,
*   so I can be yelled against,*
and stay loved. Amen.

Ministering to Parents

There once was a mother and dad
who thought they'd been tricked and been had.
They said, *"What's the use?*
We've got all this abuse."
The feeling was really quite sad.

The reason for feeling rejection
was a break in their family connection.
What made them quite wise
was the sudden surprise
that it could be healed by affection.

They looked for the good and the bad.
They listed the glad and the sad.
Then they did embrace
each list with God's grace
and erase the belief they'd been had.

Read

"Honor your father and your mother, as the Lord your God has commanded you, so that you may live long and that it may go well with you in the land the Lord your God is giving you" (Deuteronomy 5:16).

Also read: Luke 2:48-51 and Ephesians 6:1-4.

Think

● What authority has been granted to parents? What authority over teenagers does the church have? What, then, is the role of youth ministry?

● Think about how you relate to parents. Is your ministry secondary to theirs? Do you compete with family time or support it? How do parents get the information on programming that your teenagers receive?

Do

● List ways you minister to parents. Do you offer courses in family life? adolescent development? counseling? Brainstorm two new ways to help parents next year and take steps to initiate those programs.

● Plan an open house or a drop-in coffee hour for parents. Talk with them about their specific concerns.

Pray

O God, lengthen our days
'til we be full.
Lengthen our weeks
'til we be worthy.
Lengthen our years
'til we be memorable.
Lengthen our lives
'til we be finished.
Lengthen now
'til we have peace.
Lengthen our relations
'til we be family. Amen.

Dealing With Differences

Once the world held a masquerade party.
People came dressed as they wished,
and they said how this felt.
When they told what they wanted
and heard what others said,
they returned in secret to their homes.
Some were accepted for the first time.
Their disguises helped them show the truth.

Read

"Do not judge, and you will not be judged. Do not condemn, and you will not be condemned. Forgive, and you will be forgiven" (Luke 6:37).

Also read: Romans 11:11-23 and 1 Corinthians 6:1-4.

Think

● What in this scripture is hardest for you to implement in your youth ministry? What judgments do you sometimes place upon young people?

● What types of young people are most easily attracted to churches? What kinds of kids do churches find difficult to attract? How do you reach them?

Do

● Meet with two teenagers you think of as rebellious. Ask what you can do to make them feel more accepted at youth group meetings. Then ask yourself what prejudices you have toward these young people and how you can overcome those prejudices.

● Look around your meeting room. Does your youth room give the impression of a plurality of people or a single viewpoint? How can you get teenagers who are different involved with your youth group?

Pray

God, get us excited about now and here.
God, get us excited about this and that.
God, get us excited about why and how.
God, get us excited about these and those. Amen.

Positive Discipline

Once there was a school for disciples.
They came from many walks of life
and had different interests.
They wished to be followers
without losing their power to will.
To their surprise and joy
they learned to follow from inside their will.
They were led not from the front or above,
not from behind or beside,
but from within.
Their will is in tune with the will of the one
who leads them.

Read

"The fear of the Lord is the beginning of knowledge, but fools despise wisdom and discipline" (Proverbs 1:7).

Also read: Psalm 94:12 and Jeremiah 30:11.

Think

● Why does the author of Proverbs link together wisdom, discipline, knowledge and the fear of the Lord? How does God discipline us?

● Why do you discipline? How does your pattern of discipline project the message "I love you"?

Do

● After you discipline youth group members or your own children, write what happened and how you used discipline. What methods of discipline do you rely on? What attitudes about discipline are evident in your practice?

● Develop a youth group covenant that focuses on how you discipline. Include mutual expectations of leaders and kids, blessings that result from keeping the covenant, and "curses" that result when the covenant is broken.

Pray

God, when we lose control,
give us back our center.
When we go too far,
give us back our center.
When we lose our way,
give us back our center.
God, center us.
You gave us the center;
guide us from the center. Amen.

Top Priority

Once a generation lost its priorities.

When someone asked, "What's up?"

They answered, "Nothing."

They couldn't tell a diamond from plastic.

Then one of them discovered the word "oops."

It became their watchword.

From then on, when something unusual happened,

they said "oops,"

and looked at it more carefully.

Choices increased.

More and more things came alive.

They began to choose.

They made lists of things to do

and chose what was first or last.

They learned to decide.

They talked about priorities.

They compared and agreed. They disagreed.

They cheered and rallied.

They changed the order of their lists.

For some the first became the last,

and the end went to the top.

Some used calculators. Some used pencils.

Some worked best with others.

Some said "oops" alone by heart.

Read

"But what does it matter? The important thing is that in every way, whether from false motives or true, Christ is preached. And because of this I rejoice" (Philippians 1:18).

Also read: Mark 12:28-33 and 1 Corinthians 12:28.

Think

● According to Philippians 1:18, what's the top priority in ministry? Is this your youth ministry priority? What's more important?

● What aspects of your ministry are most important? People? programs? paperwork? training? How are these priorities reflected in your calendar and budget?

Do

● List on small slips of paper the tasks you do each week and attach them to children's building blocks. Stack the blocks in order of priority. Put items of the same priority at the same level. Place your highest priorities on top. What does your ministry look like now?

● Dig out your job description. Ask your senior pastor to rank your responsibilities. Ask two volunteers and three teenagers to do the same. Reflect on how their input might shape your priorities.

Pray

Jesus, you knew your priorities.
You were silent, and the world listened.
You forgave, and generations marveled.
You spoke, and the poor took heart.
You suffered, and mourners sang.
You ascended, and we hoped.
Jesus, you turned everything around. Amen

Your Christian Lifestyle

Mirrors could be used more.

We could stand before them

to make faces of feelings.

We could stand before them

with someone else and see how we look together.

We could stand before them

and see what is around and behind.

We could stand before them

and reflect and look ahead.

Mirrors could be used more.

Read

"For where your treasure is, there your heart will be also" (Matthew 6:21).

Also read: Ephesians 4:25-32.

Think

● How do people's hearts reflect their priorities and treasures? If people looked at your time, talents and treasures, where would they think your heart was? How does your life show the true treasures you've discovered in Christ?

● What does your lifestyle say about your faith? What do your teenagers learn from watching the way you live? What do they learn from the way you dress, the house you live in or the car you drive?

Do

● Tour your closet, your garage, your home. As you look through these places, write observations about your lifestyle. What might others learn from your lifestyle? Would they learn about a priority of serving Christ and caring for your family?

● Look through a Christmas catalogue. How are your priorities shown through what you purchase for Christmas gifts?

Pray

O God, keep showing us what doesn't fit,
and make us laugh or cry.
Keep showing us the ridiculous,
and make us laugh or cry.
God, keep showing us our contradictions,
and make us laugh or cry. Amen.

Encourage Christian Growth in Your Youth Group

10-MINUTE DEVOTIONS FOR YOUTH GROUPS

By J.B. Collingsworth

Get this big collection of ready-to-use devotion ideas that'll help teenagers apply God's Word to their lives. Each 10-minute faith-building devotion addresses an important concern such as ...

- Love
- Failure
- Peer pressure
- Rejection
- Faith and more ...

You'll get 52 quick devotions, each complete with scripture reference, attention-grabbing learning experience, discussion questions and a closing. Bring teenagers closer to God with these refreshing devotions— perfect for youth activities of any kind!

ISBN 0-931529-85-9 $6.95

FUN OLD TESTAMENT BIBLE STUDIES

By Mike Gillespie

Get 32 creative Old Testament Bible studies on themes important to teenagers ... forgiveness, peer pressure, temptation, friendship and more.

Each session is designed to help teenagers experience the drama of the Old Testament—then apply what they've learned to their own problems and concerns. Teach your students the meaning of ...

- Persistence—by building a precarious tower of cards
- Celebration—by creating and leading their own worship service
- Justice—by making sculptures that represent consequences of wrong actions
- Creation—by presenting a pantomime that tells the story of Creation

It's easy to help kids understand God's Word in the Old Testament. You'll get step-by-step help to prepare for each session. You'll teach Bible studies your teenagers will love! The studies come complete with ...

- Attention-grabbing openers
- Activities to help kids learn and experience scripture
- Opportunities for teenagers to grow in Christian maturity
- And ready-to-copy, fun-to-use handouts

Lead your young people toward new discoveries about God and themselves with **Fun Old Testament Bible Studies**.

ISBN 0-931529-64-6 $12.95

Exciting New Resources From

Group Books

BOREDOM BUSTERS

By Cindy S. Hansen

Boredom Busters is packed with 84 low- and no-cost activities for kids of all ages. Keep these ideas tucked up your sleeve for meetings that aren't going well. Learn how to "intentionally interrupt" a meeting with fast-paced activities.

Keep your kids' attention by . . .
- Playing human-size Tic-Tac-Toe
- Organizing an orchestra without any instruments
- Deciphering a scrambled scripture
- Batting a balloon through an obstacle course, and
- Working together to lift a teammate over a net

Don't let boredom keep your youth group from growing in faith. Instead, captivate your kids with **Boredom Busters**!

ISBN 0-931529-77-8 $7.95

QUICK CROWDBREAKERS AND GAMES FOR YOUTH GROUPS

From the editors of Group Publishing

Energize your group. Involve teenagers. Help break the ice at retreats, meetings, lock-ins—wherever you want to have a good time. Your group will enjoy the good-natured fun of these creative crowdbreakers.

Pick a game and you're set to play within minutes. No complicated preparation—ever! Most games can be played with ordinary stuff. Just follow the simple directions. Add kids. And have fun! Take your choice of . . .
- Relays . . . Banana Relay, Dog Biscuit Relay, Peel Out
- Pair games . . . Doughnut on a String, Back Art, Pingpong Plunge
- Games for teams . . . Hot-Air Football, Cookie Tower, Black Light Volleyball
- Plus zany, non-competitive activities for the whole gang . . . Group Noise Contest, Bumper Beds and many more.

Take this book wherever kids gather. You'll always be ready with a new twist for involving kids and leaders in a great time.

ISBN 0-931529-46-8 $8.95

Creative Programming Resources for Youth Ministry

DENNIS BENSON'S CREATIVE BIBLE STUDIES

By Dennis Benson

These companion volumes of imaginative Bible studies will motivate and excite your group. You get hundreds of creative studies—covering every passage in the New Testament.

These unique, ready-to-use resources give you ...

- Action-oriented learning
- Ideas to help students remember and apply what they learn to their own problems and concerns
- Cross-references from study to study
- A complete how-to-use section
- Detailed preparation tips

Get both **Creative Bible Studies**—the ready-to-use resources that build faith and make studying the Bible fun and unforgettable.

Matthew—Acts   ISBN 0-931529-01-8 $19.95
Romans—Revelation ISBN 0-931529-52-2 $12.95

INSTANT PROGRAMS FOR YOUTH GROUPS 1, 2, 3, 4

From the editors of Group Publishing

Get loads of quick-and-easy program ideas you can prepare in a flash.

Each meeting idea gives you everything you need for a dynamic program. Step-by-step instructions. Material lists of easy-to-find items. Dynamic discussion-starters and ready-to-copy handouts to involve kids.

Each book gives you 17 or more meeting ideas on topics that matter to teenagers ...

    1—Self-Image, Pressures, Living as a Christian
    2—Me and God, Responsibility, Emotions
    3—Friends, Parents, Dating and Sex
    4—Tough Topics, Faith Issues, Me and School

With all four books, you can keep a year's worth of program ideas at your fingertips—ready to tap instantly.

Instant Programs for Youth Groups 1 ISBN 0-931529-32-8 $7.95
Instant Programs for Youth Groups 2 ISBN 0-931529-42-5 $7.95
Instant Programs for Youth Groups 3 ISBN 0-931529-43-3 $7.95
Instant Programs for Youth Groups 4 ISBN 1-55945-10-X $7.95